World W  2

A World of Movement

Planet Earth

The Seashore

What is the seashore like?

The United Kingdom has one of the most varied coastlines in the world. If you went on a aeroplane ride around the coast you would see many types of seashore. There are sandy beaches, mudflats, shingle banks, rocky shores and cliffs.

▼ *A sandy beach along the Norfolk coast.*

❶

▶ *Mudflats on the River Lune estuary, Lancashire.*

▼ *A shingle bank, Chesil Beach, Dorset.*

▼ *Steep chalk cliffs at The Needles, Isle of Wight.*

▲ *A rocky coastline, Cornwall.*

Talking and writing

1 Why do people take photographs of the coast from an aeroplane? What do they use them for?

2 Write a short description of one of the photographs. Ask someone in your class to read your description and guess which picture you have chosen.

How does the sea shape the coast?

As the waves pound away at the coast they change its shape. In some places the sea wears away the land and makes cliffs and headlands. In other places it builds up beaches in sheltered bays.

Usually these changes happen very slowly and take hundreds of years. However, very rough seas can break down part of a cliff face in a few hours.

Sheltered bay

1 Sand dunes built up and shaped by the wind.

2 Sandy beach made up of very tiny pieces of rock.

3 Sheltered bay between hills.

4 Boulders worn smooth by waves.

Fact file

◆ The coast of the United Kingdom is 12,429 kilometres long.

◆ Nobody in the United Kingdom lives more than 120 kilometres from the coast.

Headland

Using the evidence

1 Look at the picture of the seashore. Which places are safe? Which places are dangerous?

2 If you visited the seashore in the picture, what activities could you do?

3 Make a geography dictionary. Draw your own pictures of the different seashore features. Write the name under each one and put them in alphabetical order.

5 Headland with cliffs juts out into the sea.

6 Caves at the bottom of the cliff.

7 Part of the cliff which has slipped into the sea.

8 Rock stack made from hard rock.

5

How do people look after the coast?

Sidmouth in Devon is a popular place in the summer months. People go there because it has a sheltered, sunny beach. There is also a cliff path for walkers. The map shows how the beach and the cliffs are looked after so visitors can enjoy them.

Things to do ✂ -----------

Make two lists showing:
(1) the ways people in Sidmouth control the sea, and
(2) the things which help people to enjoy the beach.

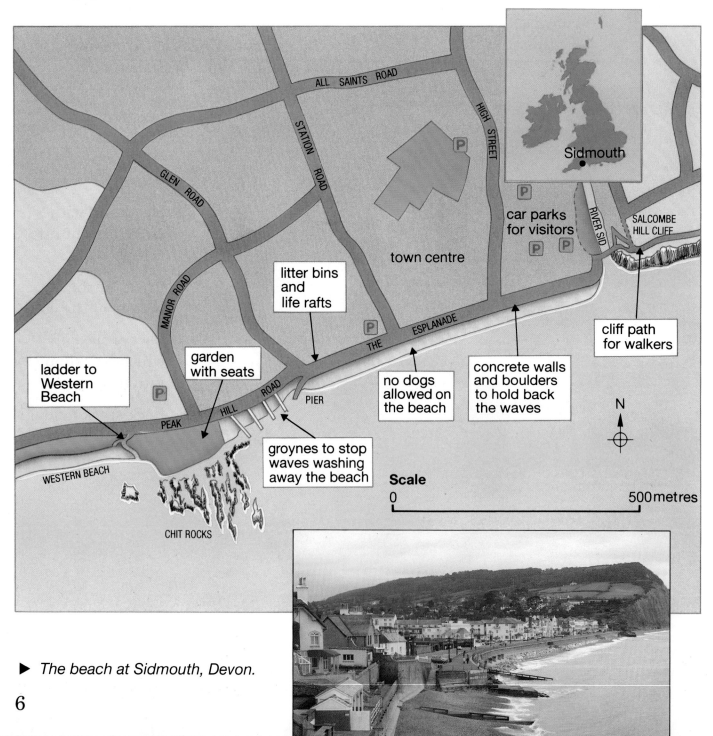

> ▶ *The beach at Sidmouth, Devon.*

What can you find on the seashore?

Lots of different plants and animals live on the seashore. The tide and the slope of the beach make different zones or habitats where they can live. The tide comes up the beach and goes out again twice a day.

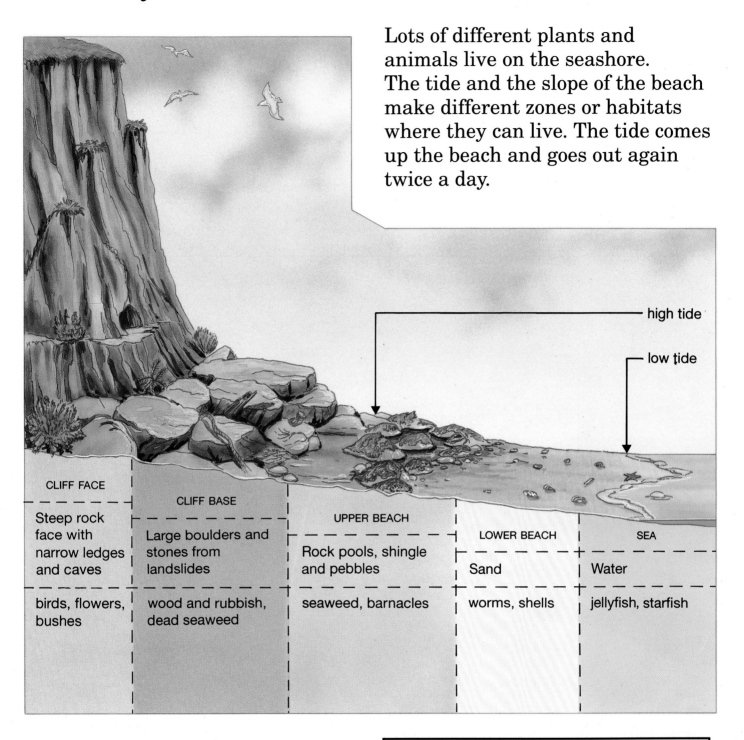

high tide

low tide

CLIFF FACE	CLIFF BASE	UPPER BEACH	LOWER BEACH	SEA
Steep rock face with narrow ledges and caves	Large boulders and stones from landslides	Rock pools, shingle and pebbles	Sand	Water
birds, flowers, bushes	wood and rubbish, dead seaweed	seaweed, barnacles	worms, shells	jellyfish, starfish

Things to do

1 Make a drawing of the beach at high tide.

2 Make up three rules to help people care for the seashore.

You have learnt

◆ there are different types of seashore
◆ how coasts are made
◆ what you can find on the seashore.

Rivers

Rivers and Valleys

What are the features of a river?

Rivers begin as tiny streams in hills and mountains. As the streams flow towards the sea they join together to make a river. Some rivers are quite short but others are thousands of kilometres long.

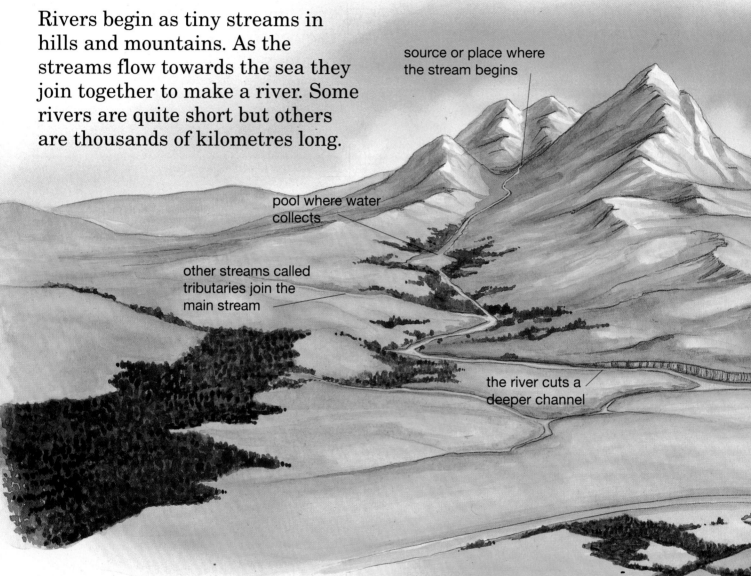

source or place where the stream begins

pool where water collects

other streams called tributaries join the main stream

the river cuts a deeper channel

Sammy the Salmon

Sammy the Salmon was born in a pool high up in the hills near where the river begins. Over the weeks he slowly grew bigger and stronger. One day he swam into the tiny stream which flowed out of the pool. He did not know why, but he felt he needed to reach the sea.

Soon Sammy felt the stream getting deeper as water drained into it from the land. The stream was turning into a river. It began to flow faster. Sammy was bounced over rocks by the rushing water and he found it difficult to breathe in the tossing foam.

When the river reached flatter land it started to meander through the countryside. Sammy swam on.

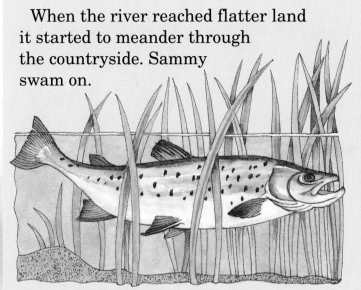

Sometimes he swam with the strong current, sometimes he rested in the shallow water by reedy banks. Sammy felt the river was changing. The river seemed to be deeper at some times of the day than others. The water even tasted different. It was salty now.

With growing excitement Sammy swam faster. He had reached the estuary with its banks of mud and small islands. Waves began to break the surface of the water. Sammy's river journey was over. He had reached the sea.

Talking and writing

1 Talk about what Sammy sees as he swims down the river.

2 Make a zigzag book of the story using the words source, tributary, channel, waterfall, meander and mouth.

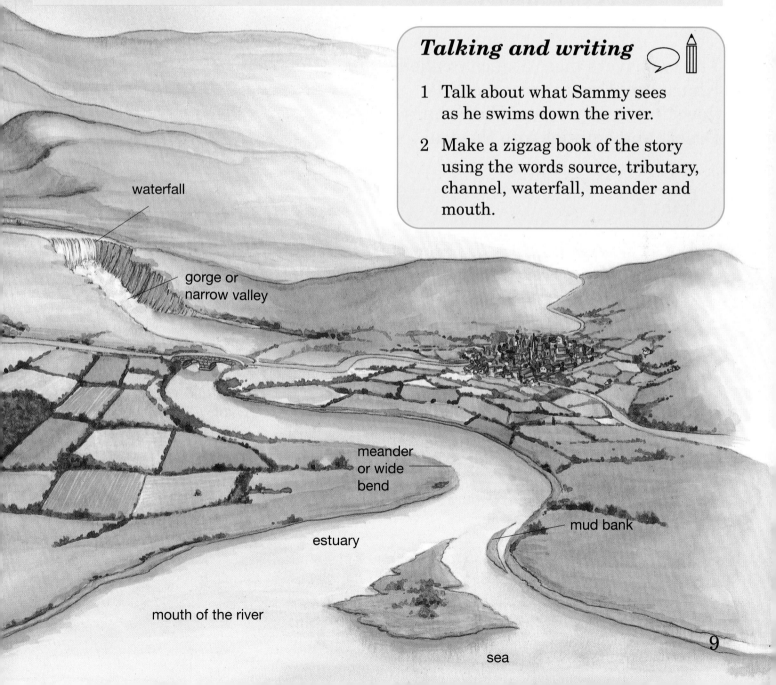

waterfall

gorge or narrow valley

meander or wide bend

mud bank

estuary

mouth of the river

sea

How do people use rivers?

The River Nile is the longest river in the world. It rises in the middle of Africa and flows north to reach the Mediterranean Sea nearly 7,000 kilometres away.

The Nile starts as two rivers. The Blue Nile rises in the mountains of East Africa. The White Nile comes from Lake Victoria. It flows over the Kabalega Falls and into the Sudd Marshes.

The two rivers meet at a city called Khartoum. From there, the Nile flows in a valley across the Sahara Desert and empties into the sea.

Fact file

◆ A lot of the water which flows into the River Nile never reaches the sea. It sinks into the ground, or evaporates into the air because of the hot temperatures in the desert.

◆ Just before the Nile meets the sea it divides into lots of small rivers. This makes a triangle of marshy land called a delta.

Using the evidence

Make a picture map for tourists showing the places they would see on a journey up the River Nile.

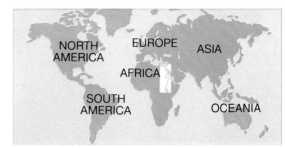

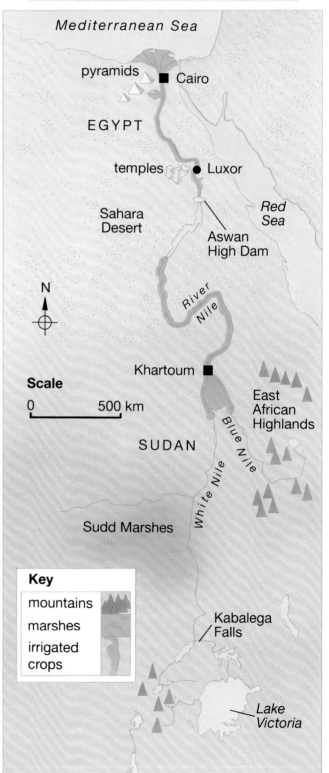

Key

mountains
marshes
irrigated crops

The River Nile brings water to the desert. For thousands of years, farmers in Egypt and the Sudan have used river water on their crops. This is called irrigation.

Many tourists visit the Nile valley. Some travel along the river by boat and visit the old temples and pyramids. Higher up the river there are huge dams which help to control floods.

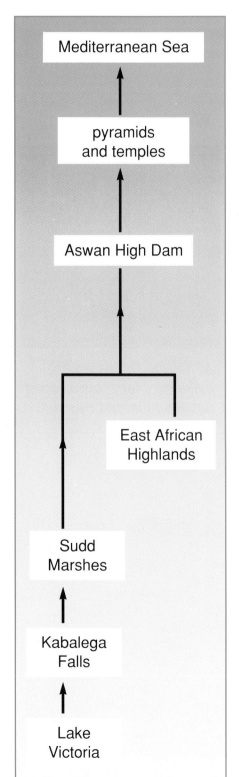

▲ *Water from the River Nile is pumped to the farmer's crops.*

▲ *Boats stop at Luxor so people can visit the ancient temples.*

▲ *The Aswan High Dam uses water from the river to make electricity.*

11

Caring for rivers

Valerie Hay works for the National Rivers Authority in the north-east of England. In her job she has to make sure that the River Tees is kept clean and healthy. These are some of the things which she does.

Things to do --------------

Write a short report about Valerie Hay's work. Say why she needs to do each task.

Monday

▲ *Testing the seawater near the mouth of the river to see if the water is clean.*

Tuesday

▲ *Dealing with an oil spill from an industrial estate.*

Wednesday

▲ *Talking to a farmer to make sure farm waste does not seep into the river.*

Thursday

▲ *Testing the water from a sewage works.*

Friday

▲ *Taking samples of river water.*

A walk along the River Thames

Children from a school in Kingston, Surrey, went on a walk along the River Thames. They wanted to find out about the special features along the river bank and to see how people use the water. These are some of the things the children saw. If your school is near a river you could make your own study.

▲ A pumping station takes water out of the river.

▲ A tug pulling a barge loaded with mud.

▲ Some people have a holiday on a river boat.

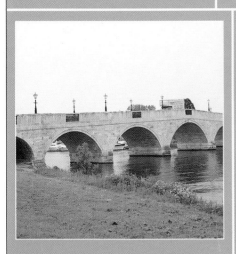

▲ Bridges help people to cross the river.

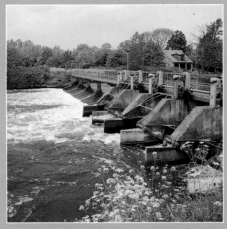

▲ Weirs control the flow of water along the river.

▲ Banks help to stop the river flooding the land.

Things to do - - - - - - - - - - - - -

Write about the different ways people use the River Thames.

You have learnt

◆ about the features of a river
◆ how people use rivers
◆ how to study a river.

Weather

Recording the Weather

How does the weather affect us?

The weather has a big effect on our lives. It affects the way we dress, the houses we live in and the things we do.

People are used to dealing with the weather. However very bad weather can sometimes cause serious problems.

The Morning Post

Blizzards in Scotland

Two walkers were found safe yesterday after heavy snow and strong winds swept across the Highlands.

THE DAILY TIMES

Hurricane hits Bermuda

Hurricane Lily hit Bermuda and the east coast of the United States yesterday. The strong winds and heavy rain caused a lot of damage.

Talking and writing

1 Divide into groups. Decide how you would describe a blizzard, a hurricane, a flood and a drought. As a class, choose the best description for each one.

2 How would each type of weather affect a tree, a house or a person? Make some drawings of your ideas.

Drought in Africa continues

There has been no rain for three months in Senegal. Farmers are losing their crops and animals are dying as water supplies dry up.

World News Monday

Floods in France

Rivers have burst their banks in northern France. The water has flooded many houses causing a lot of damage.

Fact file

◆ Eight thousand people died when a very bad storm hit southern England in 1703.

◆ Britain's longest drought was recorded in London in 1893. It lasted 73 days.

◆ The Thames Flood Barrier was opened in 1984. It was built to stop London flooding.

Who uses the weather forecast?

Most of us are interested in what the weather is going to be like. Some forecasts give information for the next few hours. Other forecasts give a more general idea of what could happen over the next week. People can choose the type of forecast they need.

Farmer

"I wonder if the weather will be good enough to get the top field harvested this week?"

Crane driver

"I need to know how strong the wind will be this afternoon."

Family

"If it's sunny tomorrow can we go for a picnic?"

Using the evidence

1 Make up a weather forecast for the farmer, crane driver and family. How will it affect what they do next?

2 Make a list of the ways people can find out about the weather forecast.

How are weather forecasts made?

Aircraft
Aircraft carry instruments that give information on the winds along their flight paths.

Balloons
Weather balloons record information as they rise through the air. They send back messages by radio.

Satellites
Weather satellites take photographs of the clouds covering the earth.

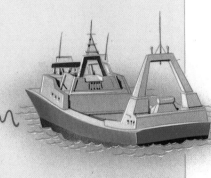

Land stations
Each day people measure the temperature, the direction of the wind and the amount of rain which has fallen.

Weather centre
All the weather information is collected together at the Bracknell Weather Centre in Berkshire and put on to maps and charts.

Ships
Ships record what the weather is like at sea.

How can we record the weather?

At St Anne's School the children decided to keep a record of the weather. First they chose the instruments they would need to measure the wind, temperature and rain. Then they kept records every day for two weeks using the symbols and words from the chart below.

▲ *The children made a weather vane to test the direction of the wind.*

Wind
There are clues which tell you about the strength of the wind.

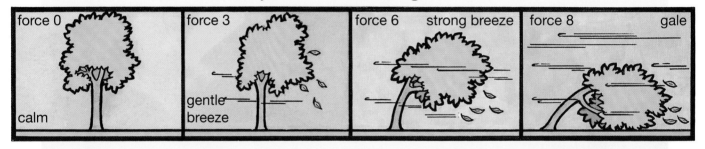

Temperature
A thermometer measures the temperature in degrees.

Cloud
Different symbols are used to show sun, cloud, rain and snow.

◀ *The data handling package on the computer showed the amount of sunshine and the temperature.*

▼ *When the children had entered all the data they printed out the results.*

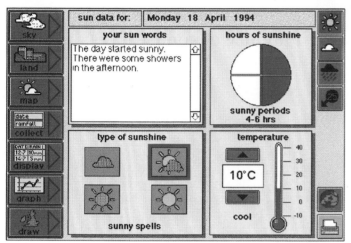 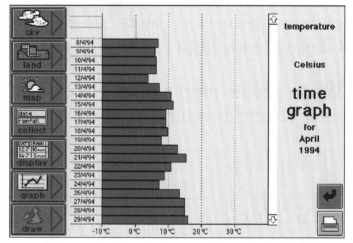

From Weathermapper © TAG Developments Ltd.

Some of the children put the information they had collected on to a computer. They used a data handling package to print out the results. When they had finished they wrote a report about the weather in their area.

Things to do ✂ - - - - - - - - - - - -

Record the weather at your school for two weeks. Show the results on a chart and write a short report. How has the weather affected the things you did?

You have learnt

- ◆ why we need weather forecasts
- ◆ how weather forecasts are made
- ◆ how you can record the weather.

Settlement

Towns

What are the features of a town?

Towns are places where lots of people live together in one place. Towns are bigger than villages but not as large as cities.

East Kilbride is a town near Glasgow in Scotland. Building the new town started in 1947. Many people who lived in old and crowded houses in the centre of Glasgow moved to the new houses.

When people plan a town they have to decide what to put in it.

These are some of the things which are needed:

◆ homes for people to live in
◆ places to work
◆ places to buy things
◆ doctors, dentists, hospitals
◆ schools and colleges
◆ ways of moving around
◆ things to do in the evenings and at weekends.

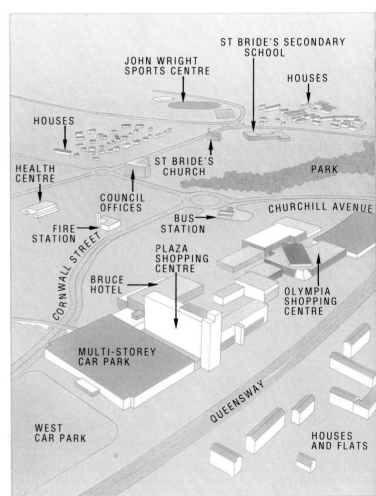

Talking and writing 🗨 ✏

1 Name the different buildings and places shown in the photograph. Use the diagram to help you.

2 Write down the number of the grid square where each building or place is found.

3 How did the town planners make sure that East Kilbride had the things people need?

▶ *East Kilbride town centre has many car parks and two shopping centres.*

East Kilbride

6

5

4

3

2

1

A   B   C   D   E   21

How did towns begin?

Many towns started off as villages. The villages grew larger because they were built at places where important routes met.

The oldest towns in the United Kingdom were started in Roman times. Later, in the Middle Ages, a lot more towns were built. Others began in Victorian times when people moved from the countryside to work in the new factories.

Towns are always changing. Today new factories and houses are usually built around the edge of a town. As jobs are created people move into the town.

Market towns

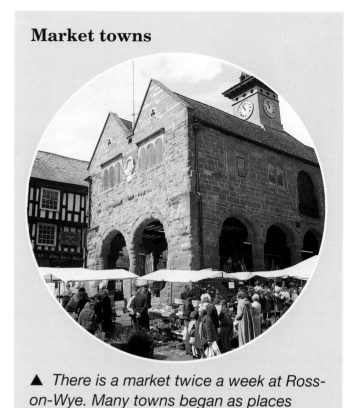

▲ *There is a market twice a week at Ross-on-Wye. Many towns began as places where people came to sell their crops and animals.*

Strong points

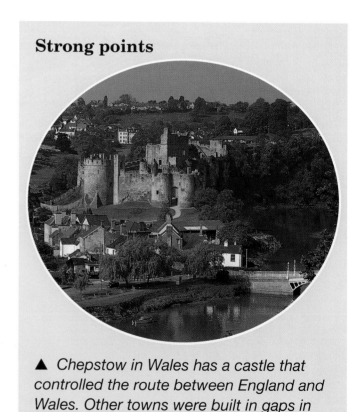

▲ *Chepstow in Wales has a castle that controlled the route between England and Wales. Other towns were built in gaps in the hills or where there was a bridge over a river.*

Using the evidence

1 Look at the photographs of the different towns. What features give you clues as to how the towns began?

2 What are the things you would expect to find in every town?

3 Using a map or atlas name five towns in your area.

Industrial towns

▲ *Thousands of people once worked in this woollen mill at Sowerby Bridge, Yorkshire. Other industrial towns were built for the people who worked in nearby factories or mines.*

Seaside resorts

▲ *Brighton in Sussex became popular for holidays because it was the easiest place by the sea to reach by road and rail from London. Seaside resorts were built for people who wanted to go to the coast for their holidays.*

Ports

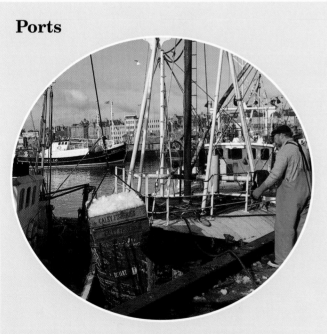

▲ *Peterhead is a port on the north-east coast of Scotland. All along the coast towns have been built around harbours where ships can load and unload their cargoes safely.*

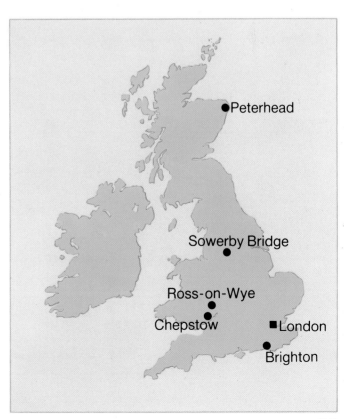

Peterhead

Sowerby Bridge

Ross-on-Wye

Chepstow

London

Brighton

How does a town work?

In the past, people who lived in the country grew their own food, collected water from the village well and gathered wood from the forest. They were able to look after their own needs.

Then more and more people started moving to the towns to find work. Water, food and other services had to be provided for them.

Things to do ✂----------------

1 Talk about the things which keep a town working. What would happen if they broke down?

2 How many of the things which keep a town running have you used today? Write a sentence or draw a picture to show how you used them.

Things which keep a modern town working

24

The children at Valley School went for a walk near their school. They looked for clues of different services.

These are some of the things they found. What clues do you think you would discover in the streets around your school?

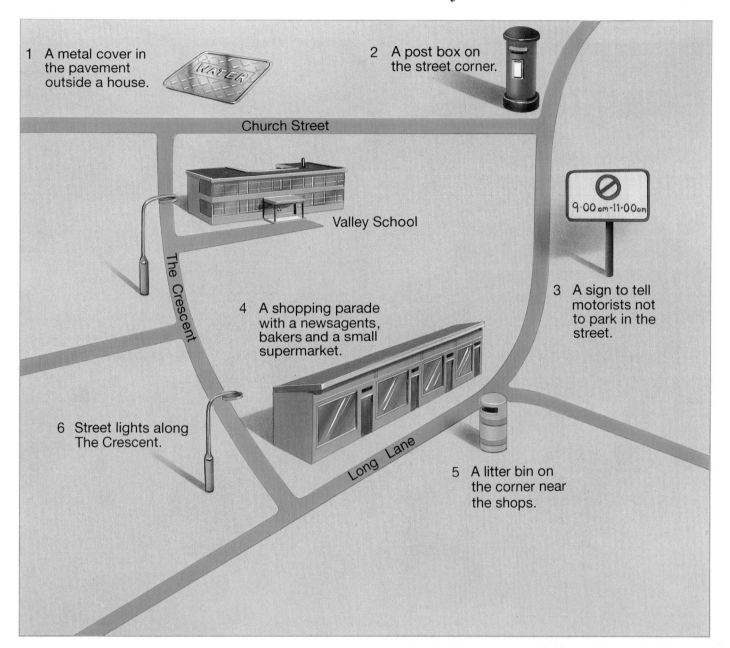

1 A metal cover in the pavement outside a house.

2 A post box on the street corner.

Church Street

Valley School

The Crescent

4 A shopping parade with a newsagents, bakers and a small supermarket.

3 A sign to tell motorists not to park in the street.

9.00am-11.00am

6 Street lights along The Crescent.

Long Lane

5 A litter bin on the corner near the shops.

Things to do - - - - - - - - - - - - - -

Think about the things the children found on their walk. How does each one help people in their daily lives?

You have learnt

- ◆ about the buildings and places in a town
- ◆ how towns grew up
- ◆ how towns provide the things people need.

Transport

Routes and Journeys

What is a route?

People spend a lot of time moving around. If you look at the school playground at playtime it is full of movement. Some children will be running here and there without thinking where they are going. Others set off with a purpose to look for a friend or a place to sit. When people make a journey they follow a route.

▲ *This photograph was taken at night. The lines of colour show the routes cars have taken.*

Paths, tracks, roads and railways provide routes for people to follow. The shortest route between two places is a straight line but marshes, hills or mountains sometimes get in the way. This forces the route to twist and bend.

Talking and writing

1 Talk about the routes you take around your school or classroom. Which ones are twisty and which ones are straight?

2 Make a list of all the things which stop routes from being completely straight.

▼ A train crossing the Ribblehead Viaduct in Yorkshire. Tunnels, viaducts and embankments help to keep railways straight and level.

▲ This road in Switzerland has to zigzag up the mountainside, otherwise cars and lorries would find the slope too steep.

▶ In some places there are special, routes for bicycles. Signposts show the route to follow.

When do people use maps?

When people travel to a place for the first time they need to think which way to go. A map helps them to plan their route.

There are many types of map. Some show the centre of a town. They are drawn to a large scale and show a lot of detail. Others mark things like railway lines. They are drawn to a smaller scale and are not as detailed.

People who are driving, walking or travelling by train look for the best map which shows their route. They can measure the distance using the scale bar.

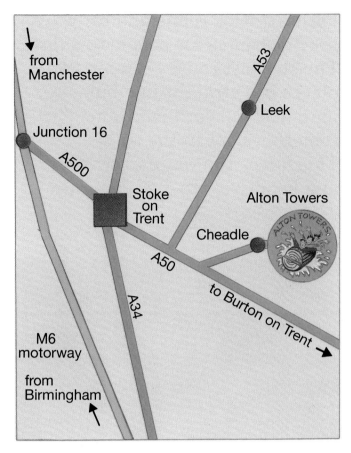

▲ *How to find Alton Towers in Staffordshire.*

Van driver

"When I am delivering goods to schools, I need a map which shows street names, roundabouts and other landmarks."

Walker

"When I am planning a walking trip, I use a map which marks the hills, footpaths, bridges and villages."

Train passenger

"When I am travelling by train, I need a map which shows me how I can get from one place to another."

Street maps
A grid of small squares makes it easier to find places on a street map.

Footpath maps
Many footpath maps are made by the Ordnance Survey. They show buildings and the shape of the land.

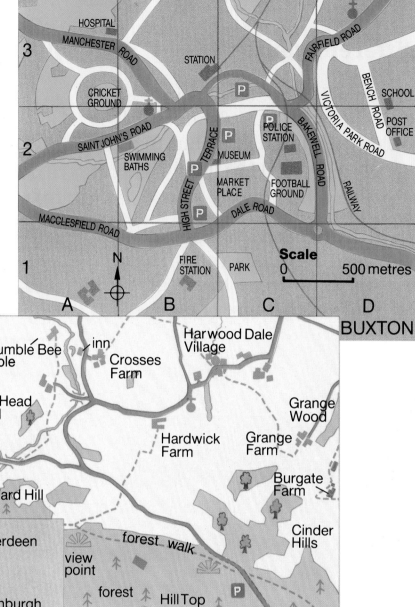

BUXTON

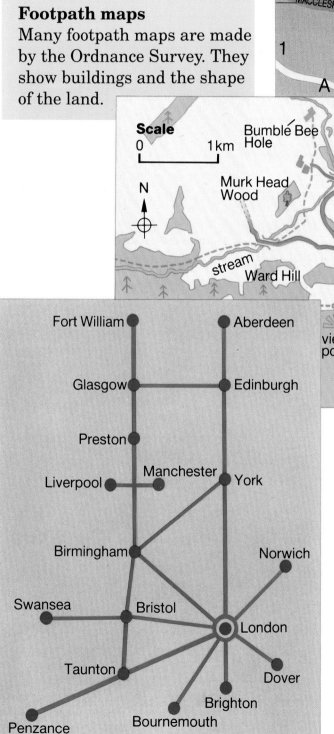

© Crown Copyright

Train maps
Train maps show rail routes between places.

Using the evidence

1 Which sort of map would the driver, walker or train passenger use and why?

2 Make a list of the main features shown on each map.

Different routes

Burydale Junior School is in Stevenage in Hertfordshire. Each week the children go by bus to the swimming pool in the middle of the town.

Normally the driver takes the route past Fairlands Valley Park. One week the driver had to go a different way because of road works.

Mapwork

Make some drawings of the different things the children see on each route. Put the drawings in order and add arrows to make a route diagram.

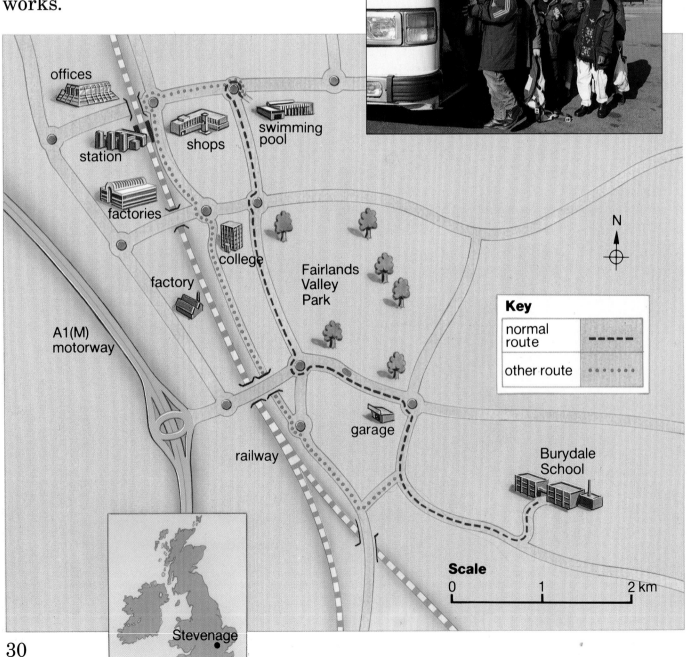

offices

station

shops

swimming pool

factories

college

factory

A1(M) motorway

Fairlands Valley Park

garage

railway

Burydale School

N

Key

| normal route | - - - - - |
| other route | · · · · · · · |

Scale

0   1   2 km

Stevenage

As part of their project on 'Routes' the children talked about their journeys from home to school.

They made a list of the landmarks which they passed and then drew maps of their journeys.

my school

+ Church

Oaks Cross

Shops

h h h

garages

h

h

My Route from school to my house

N

W   E

S

h h h

my house

Things to do ✂ --------------

1 Make a list of the landmarks you pass on your way from home to school. Show them on a map of your route.

2 Do you come to school by car, by bus, or on foot? Collect information from other children and make a class bar chart.

You have learnt

◆ what a route is
◆ how people use maps for journeys
◆ the importance of landmarks.

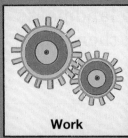

Work

Making Things

Where are things made?

Most of the things that we eat, wear and use each day are made in factories. Some factories are very small places with one or two workers. Others employ thousands of people and take up as much space as a small town.

▲ *This chemical works at Whitehaven in Cumbria makes materials which are used to make soap, toothpaste and cement.*

▲ *Small workshops, like this sign maker, are sometimes found in quiet side streets.*

▲ *Larger factory units, like this brickworks, are usually built on industrial estates.*

All factories are made up of various parts. They need:

◆ workshops, offices and storage space
◆ a main entrance, a delivery area and a car park
◆ a way of supplying power for machines
◆ a way of getting rid of waste.

Talking and writing

1 Why do factories need the different parts shown in the picture below?

2 What are the differences between a factory and your school? Is anything the same?

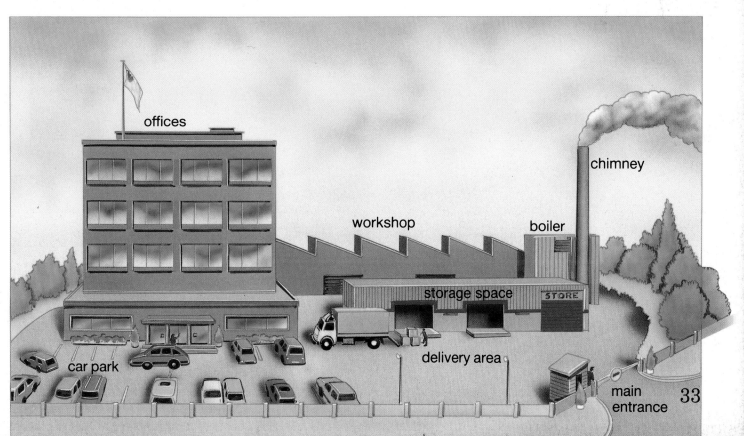

offices

chimney

workshop

boiler

storage space

STORE

delivery area

car park

main entrance

How do factories work?

Before a factory can make anything it needs raw materials. These materials are either dug out of the earth or produced by farmers and fishermen. Factories turn the raw materials into the goods we see in shops.

Factories use machines to make things quickly and cheaply. Machines can make large numbers of things in exactly the same way each time.

Making bread
Input-output diagram

Input	*What happens*	*Output*
flour yeast salt water	mixing shaping baking	loaves of bread

Using the evidence

Make input-output diagrams to show how glass and spoons are made.

Making bread

Bread is made from flour, yeast, salt and water.

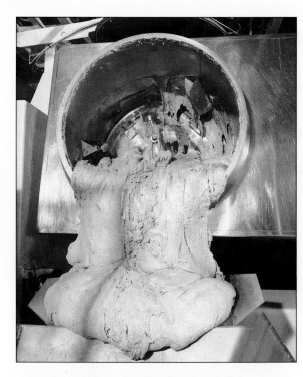

The ingredients are mixed together to make a dough.

INPUT　　　　　　　　**WHAT HAPPENS**

Making glass bowls

Glass is made from sand, washing soda and limestone. The raw materials are mixed together and heated in a furnace until they melt. The red hot glass is then rolled into sheets or shaped to make bottles, jars, bowls and other items.

Making spoons

Spoons are made from stainless steel. The steel is cut into strips, pressed into the right shape and then polished.

The dough is shaped into loaves ready to be baked in the oven.

The bread is sliced, wrapped, put into crates and sent to shops.

WHAT HAPPENS ➔ **OUTPUT** ➔

What do factories make?

Bricks and spoons are made in factories in one piece. Other things, like pens or bikes, are made from different parts called components.

Components are made from different materials. Some materials are chosen because they are strong, or because they bend easily.

Things to do ✂ --------------

Copy the lists of the components for a bicycle and a pair of trainers. Why have the materials used for each component been chosen?

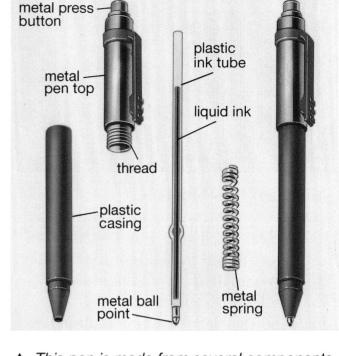

▲ *This pen is made from several components.*

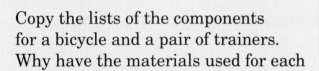

Outdoor activity
Modern styling
Durable sole

Main components
rubber sole
leather top, or uppers
plastic eyeholes
cotton laces
plastic label
cotton stitching
foam rubber lining

Main components
rubber tyres
metal frame
plastic seat
rubber hand grips
glass reflectors
metal chain
metal brake cables

◀▶ *Advertisements tell us about things made in factories.*

handles
Plastic

screw
metal

blade
metal

Christopher Godwin R4

The children at St Mark's School made a list of the things in their classroom which were made in a factory. They looked at some of them very carefully and then made drawings of the components. You could do the same.

You have learnt

◆ what a factory looks like
◆ about inputs and outputs
◆ that some goods are made from components.

Environment

Caring for Towns

Why do we need to look after buildings?

Most of us think that the house where we live and streets where we grow up are special in some way. However buildings wear out. Most old buildings are knocked down and replaced by new ones. A few are saved because they are interesting or important for their history.

Talking and writing

1 Why do you think the block of flats is being knocked down? What could be built in its place?

2 Discuss how the buildings in the photographs on page 39 have been altered so they can be useful today.

▶ *Manchester Exhibition Centre was once a railway station.*

◀ *These buildings in Chester have been used as shops for hundreds of years.*

▶ *Some windmills, like this one in Essex, have been turned into houses.*

How can places be improved?

Duncan Brown works as a town planner in Glasgow. He decides how to make the streets and other places as pleasant as possible. Duncan spends a lot of time out of doors making surveys and taking photographs.

When he goes back to his office at the council buildings he makes drawings and writes reports about the changes which could be made. He also works out how much the changes would cost. The council then asks local people what they think of Duncan's ideas. This gives everyone a chance to improve the place where they live.

▼ *These 'Before' and 'After' pictures show how a lot of small changes can make a big difference.*

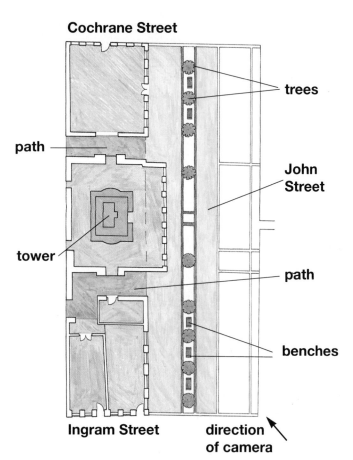

Before

After

Using the evidence

1 Look at the two photographs Make a list of the changes Duncan has suggested.

2 How do these changes make the street a pleasanter place?

Improvement schemes

Traffic calming

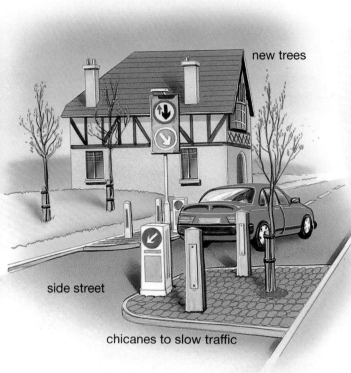

new trees

side street

chicanes to slow traffic

New play equipment

climbing frame

soft tarmac

bright colours

shelter for passengers

street lights

car park

good bus service to town centre

Park and ride

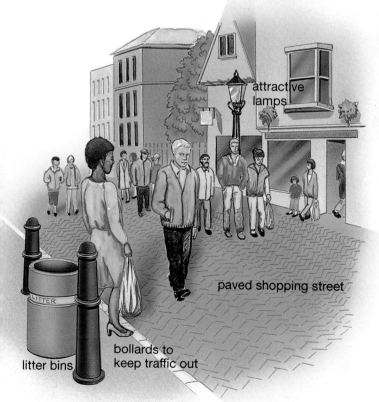

attractive lamps

paved shopping street

litter bins

bollards to keep traffic out

Pedestrianisation

Using the evidence

1 How does each of the schemes in the pictures improve the environment? Write a short report.

2 Make up a set of questions you could use in a survey about improving the streets near your school.

Which place is best?

All over the country there are competitions for the best kept towns and villages. When the judges visit each place they have a list of questions. They give marks to various features to decide which town will win the award.

Buildings	**Town A**	**Town B**

Are the buildings in good repair?

◆ walls
◆ roofs
◆ gutters
◆ paintwork
◆ windows

Pollution	**Town A**	**Town B**

Is the place clean or dirty?

◆ litter
◆ dog's mess
◆ graffiti
◆ oil stains
◆ fumes

Street furniture	Town A	Town B

Are there enough things to help people?

- ◆ seats
- ◆ lights
- ◆ signs
- ◆ telephone boxes
- ◆ post boxes

Appearance	Town A	Town B

Is the place pleasant or unpleasant?

- ◆ overhead wires
- ◆ advertisements
- ◆ plants and trees
- ◆ satellite dishes
- ◆ noise

Things to do ✂

1. Look at each pair of photographs and decide which town would score the highest marks. Do you think Town A or Town B would win the award?

2. Do a survey of your own area. Make drawings or take photographs of good and bad things near your school.

You have learnt

- ◆ how old buildings can be given new uses
- ◆ how people look after towns and villages
- ◆ how to compare different environments.

Northern Ireland

United Kingdom

What is Northern Ireland like?

Northern Ireland is the smallest country in the United Kingdom. It lies to the west of Scotland across the Irish Sea.

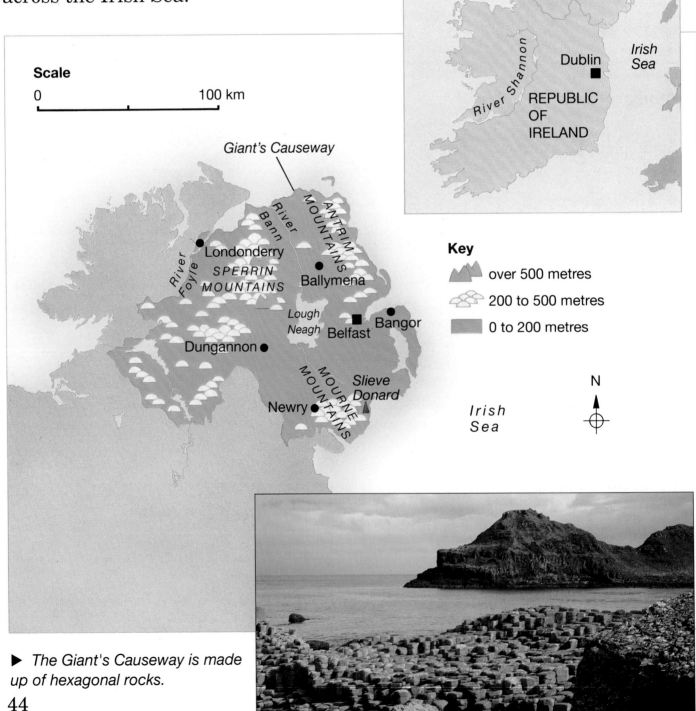

Scale

0   100 km

Giant's Causeway

River Bann

ANTRIM MOUNTAINS

River Foyle

Londonderry

SPERRIN MOUNTAINS

Ballymena

Lough Neagh

Belfast

Bangor

Dungannon

MOURNE MOUNTAINS

Slieve Donard

Newry

Atlantic Ocean

NORTHERN IRELAND

Belfast ■

River Shannon

Dublin ■

Irish Sea

REPUBLIC OF IRELAND

Key

△ over 500 metres

☁ 200 to 500 metres

▬ 0 to 200 metres

Irish Sea

N

▶ The Giant's Causeway is made up of hexagonal rocks.

44

Rivers and landscape

The River Bann is the longest river. Gently rolling countryside covers most of Northern Ireland. In some places there are rugged hills and mountains.

Weather

West winds from the Atlantic Ocean bring a lot of rain. The wind also affects the temperature. In summer it is cool but there is not much snow in winter.

Settlement

▲ *Belfast town centre and docks.*

Belfast is the capital of Northern Ireland and the only large city in the country. Londonderry, Bangor and Newry are smaller towns around the coast. Most people live in the countryside in small villages and on farms.

Talking and writing

Design a set of four postage stamps showing different aspects of Northern Ireland.

Fact file

- ◆ Slieve Donard (852 metres) is the highest mountain in Northern Ireland.

- ◆ Lough Neagh is the largest lake in the United Kingdom.

- ◆ Ireland is called the Emerald Isle because of the green landscape.

Work

Ships have been made in Belfast for many years. There is also work in factories making aircraft, food and clothes, but some people are unemployed. In the country, farmers produce meat, eggs and butter.

Transport

Road and rail routes spread out from Belfast. Two motorways connect Belfast to the nearby towns of Ballymena and Dungannon. Planes and ferries link Northern Ireland with other parts of the United Kingdom.

▲ *Annalong harbour in County Down.*

Living in Northern Ireland

Cathy O'Neill   Michael O'Neill   Mr O'Neill   Mrs O'Neill

Cathy and Michael O'Neill live at Ballyknock Farm in County Londonderry. Their parents spend most of the time running the farm. Mrs O'Neill also has a part time job in a clothes factory about six kilometres away.

Cathy and Michael go to school in Maghera. On school days a bus comes to collect them at 8.00 am. There are about 350 children in the school. Most of them live in the countryside around Maghera.

▲ The barns on the farm are used for storing hay.

▲ Glen Primary School.

◄ On the way home the bus stops near to the children's homes.

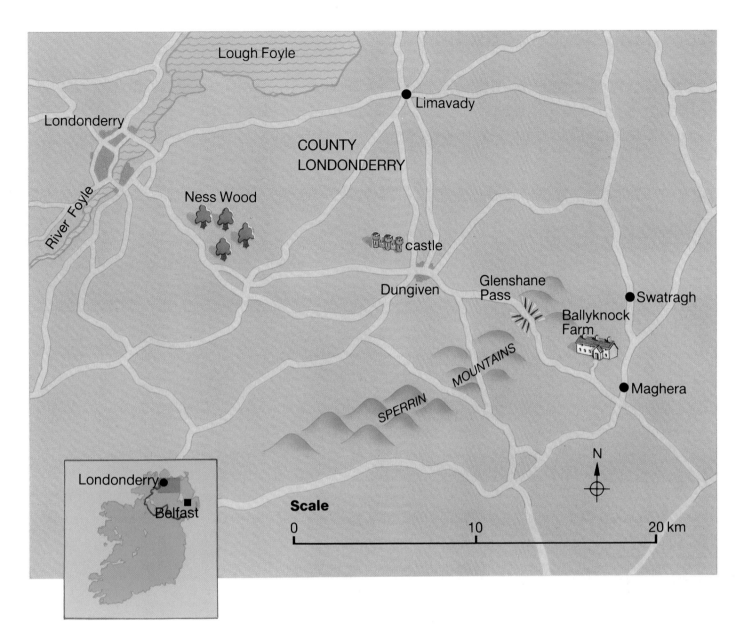

After school Cathy and Michael help their parents on the farm. Sometimes they collect the cows for milking. In the summer they help to harvest the grass in the fields. They often have to wear their anoraks because it rains a lot in Northern Ireland.

Ballyknock Farm is about two kilometres from the main road which goes to Londonderry and Belfast. Some years ago the road was widened so it could take more traffic. From the farm you can see the road winding up the hill to the Glenshane Pass which takes traffic through the Sperrin Mountains.

Cathy and Michael have lived at Ballyknock Farm all their lives. Mr and Mrs O'Neill like the peace of the countryside but sometimes Cathy and Michael wish more of their friends lived nearby.

A journey to Londonderry

On Saturdays the O'Neills sometimes go shopping in Londonderry. The journey takes about 45 minutes. The drawings show some of the things they see on the way.

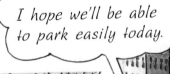

▲ *The River Foyle and Londonderry, or Derry as some people call it.*

◄ *Shipquay Street, Londonderry.*

Londonderry is an important town. It has lots of factories and shops and a large hospital. Ships sail up the River Foyle to unload their goods at the port.

Cathy and Michael like coming to Londonderry. Sometimes their father takes them to the cinema.

Things to do

1 If you lived at Ballyknock Farm what would you like and dislike?

2 Write a diary entry about Cathy and Michael's trip to Londonderry.

You have learnt

◆ about the landscape and weather of Northern Ireland
◆ about the work people do
◆ how people live in the countryside.

Germany

What is Germany like?

Europe

Germany lies to the east of the United Kingdom across the North Sea. More people live in Germany than in any other country in Europe. For many years Germany was divided into two parts. It was united in 1990.

▼ *A deep gorge along the River Rhine.*

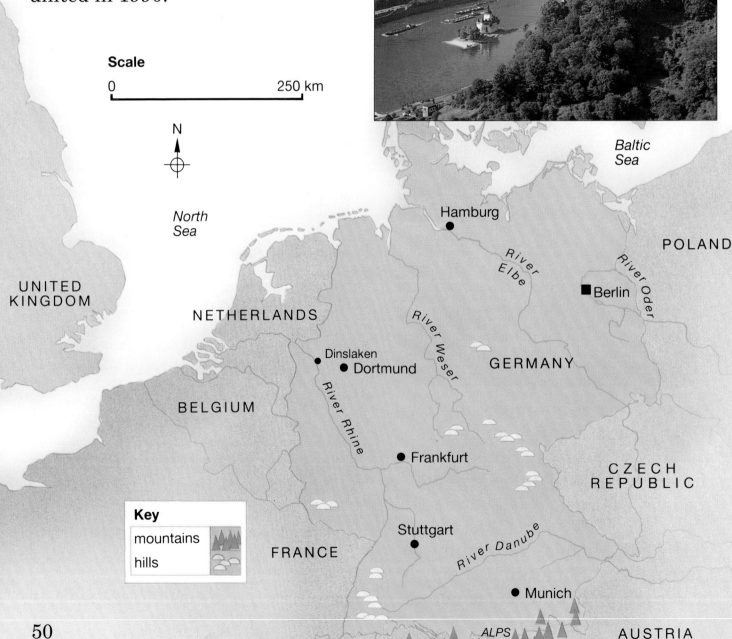

Scale

0   250 km

N

North Sea

Baltic Sea

POLAND

UNITED KINGDOM

NETHERLANDS

Hamburg

River Elbe

River Oder

Berlin ■

Dinslaken

Dortmund

River Weser

GERMANY

BELGIUM

River Rhine

Frankfurt

CZECH REPUBLIC

Key

mountains

hills

FRANCE

Stuttgart

River Danube

Munich

ALPS

AUSTRIA

Rivers and landscape

The Rhine, Weser, Elbe, Danube and Oder are the main rivers. Northern Germany is very flat. Central and southern Germany have more hills.

Settlement

Berlin is the capital city of Germany. Hamburg is the main port. Munich, Stuttgart, Frankfurt and Dortmund are other large cities. Most people in Germany live in towns and cities.

▼ *The Brandenburg Gate, Berlin.*

Work

Germany used to be famous for coal mining and for making steel. Today it makes machinery, cars and chemicals. Western Germany has many factories, banks and offices. Eastern Germany is slowly being modernised.

Weather

In the winter, Germany is usually colder than the United Kingdom. Most places have less wind than the United Kingdom because they are further from the sea.

▼ *Wurst are a type of sausage. They are very popular in Germany.*

Transport

Germany was the first country to build a network of motorways in the 1930s. It also has a new high speed train system.

Talking and writing

What would you put in a fact file about Germany?

A visit to Germany

Dominic is nine years old. He lives with his mother and father in Durham in the north of England. His mother was born in Germany so the family often go there for their holidays.

Dominic's grandmother, uncles, aunts and cousins live in Dinslaken. It is one of a group of towns on the River Rhine about 500 kilometres south-west of Berlin.

The journey from Dominic's home in Durham to Dinslaken takes a whole day. Dominic and his family have to leave home very early in the morning and drive to Harwich in Essex where they catch a ferry. The crossing to the Hook of Holland takes seven hours. From there they take the motorway across the Netherlands and into Germany.

Durham   Harwich   Hook of Holland   Dinslaken

Dinslaken

Just over 60,000 people live in Dinslaken. At the centre of the town there is a busy shopping street. During the summer it is warm enough to sit outside and have a drink at one of the cafés.

▲ *The main shopping street is pedestrianised.*

There are many large buildings in Dinslaken, such as the town hall, sports centre, college, churches and banks. There are also markets where fresh fruit and vegetables are sold everyday. Some of these products are grown on nearby farms.

Many people from the town work in the coal mine and the steel works. Recently some people have lost their jobs because there is not as much work as there used to be. A lot of people also work for a large firm called Pintsch Bamag. It makes signals for roads, railways, ships and aircraft.

▲ *When Dominic and his family come to Dinslaken they stay at his grandmother's house.*

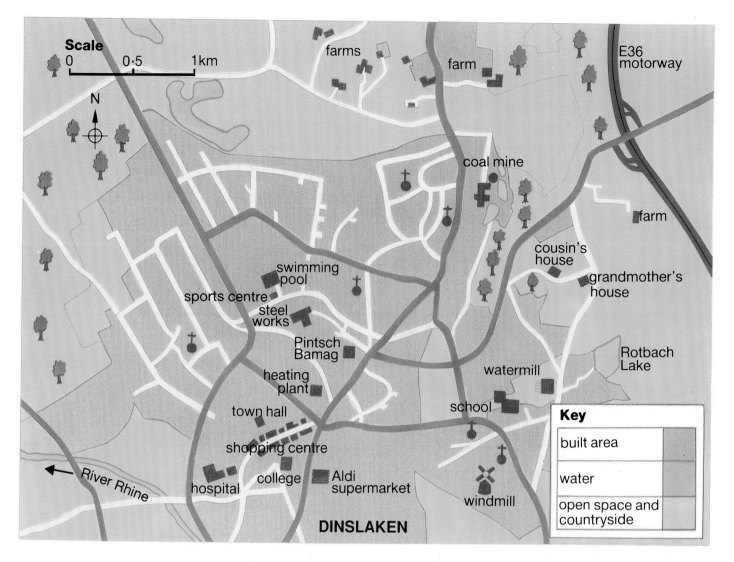

Scale
0   0.5   1km

N

farms
farm
E36
motorway

coal mine

farm

cousin's
house

grandmother's
house

swimming
pool

sports centre

steel
works

Pintsch
Bamag

heating
plant

town hall

shopping centre

hospital   college   Aldi
supermarket

watermill

school

Rotbach
Lake

windmill

River Rhine

DINSLAKEN

Key

built area	
water	
open space and countryside	

While Dominic is in Dinslaken he always visits his cousins, Martin and Andrea. Martin is ten years old and he goes to school nearby. In Germany children start school when they are seven. Andrea is only six so she goes to a nursery called a kindergarten.

Martin and Andrea's parents both have jobs. Their father is a manager at the local Aldi supermarket. Their mother is a nurse. She works in the accident unit at the hospital. Sometimes people are brought into the hospital by ambulance because of an accident on the motorway which passes close to Dinslaken.

When Dominic visits his cousins in the summer they often go to Rotbach Lake for a picnic. The lake is just outside Dinslaken. People go there to ride their bikes, sail, go fishing, play ball games or walk in the woods.

In the winter holidays they go ice skating or watch an ice hockey match. Sometimes they go to the indoor swimming pool.

Changes and differences

Each time Dominic visits Dinslaken he notices changes. Some of the old factories have been pulled down and new ones put up. A heating plant has been built to burn the town's rubbish. This makes heat which is piped to new houses nearby.

Sometimes Dominic looks out of the window of his grandmother's house and thinks of his home in England. The houses are not quite the same shape here, the signs are all written in German and there are no hedges to the fields. It is also colder in winter. Things are a little bit different in Germany.

▲ *The old watermill has been made into a museum.*

▲ *In Germany, Dominic always has cold meats for breakfast. There is usually a choice of different cheeses, bread and hot rolls as well.*

Things to do  --------------

1 Make a diagram map of the route from Durham to Dinslaken showing times and distances.

2 What would Dominic see on the journey from Durham to Dinslaken? Use an atlas to help you.

3 Make a list of the places shown on the map of Dinslaken. Who might use each one?

4 Design a postcard showing different features of Dinslaken.

You have learnt

◆ about the landscape and weather in Germany
◆ how people live
◆ what work people do.

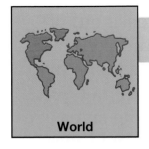

Central and North America

What are Central and North America like?

The landscape of Central and North America is very varied. Mexico and Central America have large rainforests. The United States of America has grasslands, deserts and mountains. Northern Canada has lots of snow and ice in winter and a very short summer.

The American Indians and Inuit have lived in Central and North America for thousands of years. More recently people from Europe, Africa and Asia have also made their homes there.

▲ *New York has many famous skyscrapers.*

▲ *The Rocky Mountains stretch down North America from Canada to Mexico.*

▲ *The Maya Indians built this pyramid in the Mexican rainforest 3,000 years ago.*

56

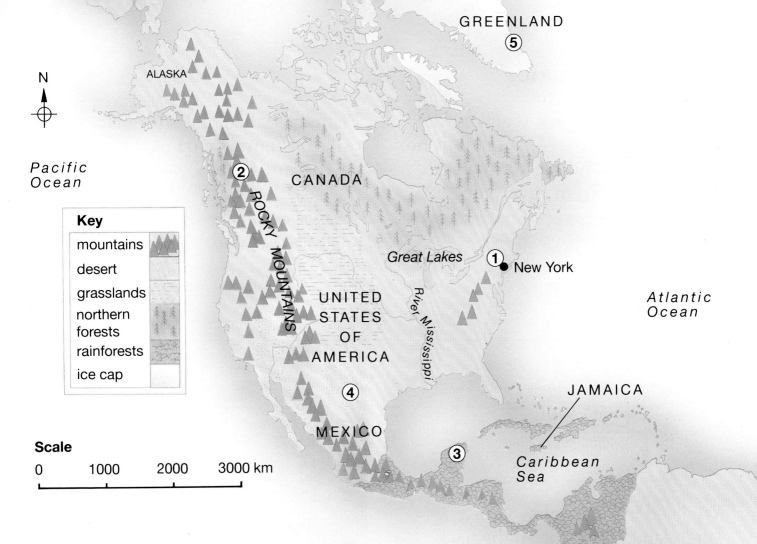

N

ALASKA

Pacific
Ocean

CANADA

ROCKY MOUNTAINS

UNITED
STATES
OF
AMERICA

MEXICO

GREENLAND
⑤

Great Lakes

①● New York

River Mississippi

JAMAICA

Atlantic
Ocean

Caribbean
Sea

②

④

③

Key

mountains	
desert	
grasslands	
northern forests	
rainforests	
ice cap	

Scale

0   1000   2000   3000 km

▲ Huge cactus plants grow in the Arizona Desert in the United States.

▲ In Greenland people can only live around the coast.

Talking and writing

Decide where each of the photographs was taken. Look at the numbers on the map to help you.

Living in Jamaica

Ingrid Morrison is a teacher. She was brought up in Jamaica but has lived in England for many years. The children from Riverside Primary School asked Ingrid to talk to them as part of their project on Distant Places.

> I was brought up in Claremont. This is a town in the north of Jamaica about half an hour by car from the coast.

We lived in a bungalow with a verandah in the front. At the back there was an orchard where we kept chickens, cows and goats.

▲ There are trees all around the bungalow.

In the fields all around us people grew sugar cane, bananas, oranges and lots of other fruits. They also grew vegetables like yams, sweet potatoes and peppers.

School started at 7.30 in the morning so we could have our lessons before it got too hot. I wore a tunic and white blouse for school. The boys wore khaki trousers and white shirts.

▲ A field of sugar cane.

What is Jamaica like?

Jamaica is an island in the Caribbean Sea. It is about half the size of Wales. Around the coast there are sandy beaches and palm trees. The highest point is Blue Mountain Peak which is 2,258 metres high.

Jamaica is much hotter than the United Kingdom. There are only two seasons. From November until April it is fairly dry. Then from May to October it is much wetter.

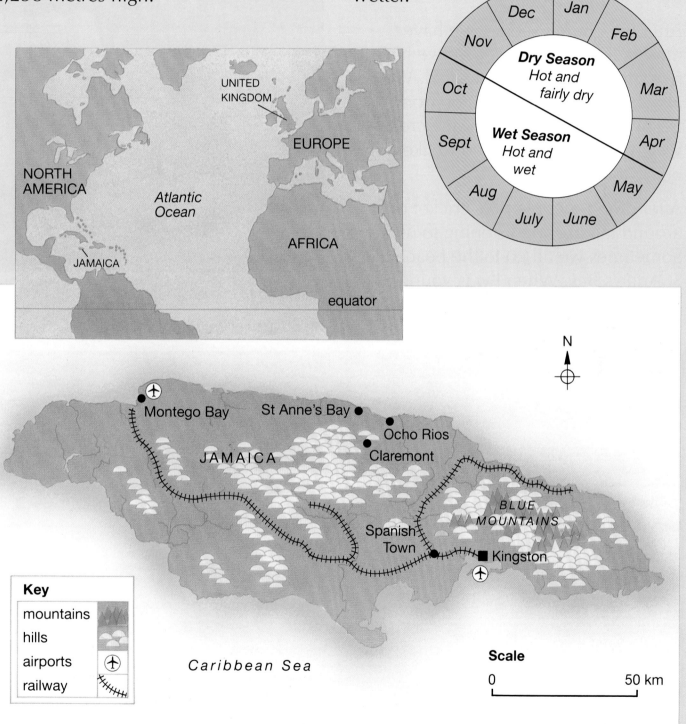

UNITED KINGDOM

EUROPE

NORTH AMERICA

Atlantic Ocean

JAMAICA

AFRICA

equator

Dec | Jan
Nov | Feb
Oct | Mar
Dry Season Hot and fairly dry
Sept | Apr
Wet Season Hot and wet
Aug | May
July | June

N

Montego Bay

St Anne's Bay

Ocho Rios

JAMAICA

Claremont

BLUE MOUNTAINS

Spanish Town

Kingston

Caribbean Sea

Key

mountains
hills
airports
railway

Scale

0   50 km

Sunday in Jamaica

Sunday is the best day of the week in Jamaica. In the morning everybody puts on their smartest clothes and goes to church. The women and girls all wear hats and the men put on their suits.

After the church service we have dinner. For the main course we have rice, beans, chicken and salad. We also have a cool drink made from freshly squeezed fruit and ice cream. When I was a child I used to like this better than anything else.

After dinner people play cricket or sit around talking and listening to music. Sometimes we all go to the beach at St Anne's Bay. When I was young I used to look for new shells for my collection.

▲ *Going to church.*

▼ *Sunday afternoon on the beach.*

Jamaica today

Claremont has changed quite a bit since I was young. There are many more houses now. Also people have more possessions like TVs and videos.

Tourists from Europe and North America come to Jamaica for their holidays. They fly to the airport at Kingston or Montego Bay and stay at hotels along the coast. The tourists bring money but the seashore is being damaged. Mangrove forests are cleared away to make room for new buildings. Parrots and other animals which live in the forests are losing their habitats.

▲ *On the edge of big towns some people have built their own homes.*

▲ *Today yellow-billed parrots are very rare in Jamaica.*

In the towns many people work in clothes factories. Some people cannot find work and are very poor. They live in houses made of old sheets of metal, cardboard and other things which have been thrown away.

When I first came to England everything seemed very different. I found the weather very cold. English people stay indoors much more. In Jamaica we are always going outside and meeting our friends. I have got used to it now.

Things to do - - - - - - - - - - - - - -

1 What questions do you think the children asked Ingrid about Jamaica? Write down your ideas.

2 How is Jamaica (a) similar, and (b) different from the United Kingdom?

You have learnt

◆ about the landscape of Central and North America
◆ about everyday life in Jamaica
◆ how people can tell you about a place.

Glossary

blizzard	A heavy snow storm with strong winds.
coast	Where the land and sea meet.
components	Parts which are put together in a factory to make a finished product.
continent	A large block of land, such as Africa.
delta	A triangular shaped area of flat land at the mouth of a river.
desert	A dry area where there is very little rain.
drought	A period of dry weather without rain.
environment	The world around us.
equator	An imaginary line around the earth, half-way between the north and south poles.
estuary	The place where a river widens as it meets the sea.
factory	A place where goods are made so they can be sold.
flood	Water covering land that is normally dry, often causing people problems.
fumes	Gases which damage the health of people, plants and animals.
graffiti	Unwanted writing and painting on walls and buildings.
habitat	The place where plants and animals live.
hurricane	Fierce storms with high winds which usually happen near the equator.
industrial estate	A place where factories and warehouses are grouped together.
irrigation	Supplying water to plants using a system of ditches or pipes.
landmarks	Buildings, mountains and other features which stand out from their surroundings.
meander	A large bend in a river.
pollution	Changes in our surroundings which damage the health of people, plants or animals.
raw materials	Things we use which come from the earth, plants or animals.
rainforest	Areas of thick forest which are near the equator.
route	A way of getting from one place to another.
scale bar	A measured line on a map from which the real distance between places can be worked out.
seashore	The land affected by the action of the sea, such as cliffs, beaches and mudflats.
services	Things which are provided for people to use, such as piped water, electricity, schools and hospitals.
settlement	The places where people live, such as villages, towns and cities.
source	The place where a river begins, such as a pool, marsh or underground spring.
tide	The rise and fall of the sea up and down the seashore.
United Kingdom	The country made up of England, Wales, Scotland and Northern Ireland.
weather forecast	What the weather is expected to be like in the days ahead.
zone	A small area of land.

Index

Published in 1995 by Collins Educational
An imprint of HarperCollins*Publishers*
77-85 Fulham Place Road
Hammersmith
London W6 8JB

www.**Collins**Education.com
On-line support for schools and colleges

Reprinted 2000

98765

ISBN 0 00 315 471 8

Printed by printing Express Ltd, Hong Kong

Design by Chi Leung

Picture research by Faith Perkins

Photographs reproduced by permission of:
(t=top, b=bottom, l=left, r=right, c=centre)
J Allan Cash pp11c, 22t; Ardea (Dennis Avon) p61l; Anna Aston pp53l&r, 55l; Colin Bridge p33l; British Shoe Corporation 36bl; Celtic Picture Library p22b; City of Glasgow Planning Department p40; Stephanie Colasanti pp58tr&bl; Colorific (Michael Yamashita) p2c; Corning Consumer Ltd p35tl; James Davis Travel Photography p60b; G Dempsey p46; East Kilbride District Council (Aerofilms) p21; European Flyers p2t; The Federation of Bakers p34l; The Flour Advisory Bureau Ltd pp34r&35; Greater Manchester Exhibition and Event Centre (Paul Francis Photography) p39b; Halfords p36r; Robert Harding Picture Library pp14t&b, 44, 51r, 57r, 60t; Terry Jewson pp3b, 18, 27b, 30, 37t, 42-43, 53; National Rivers Authority p12; Northern Ireland Tourist Board Picture Library p45b, 49t&b; Christine Osborne Pictures pp11t&b; PANOS Pictures (Jeremy Hartley) p15l, 61r; Popperfoto p15r; Rex Features p38; Science Photo Library (Simon Fraser) p32; Stephen Scoffham pp6, 19, 31, 33r, 42-43, 58tl; Slide File p45t; Spectrum pp3cl, 23tr, 27tl; Still Moving Picture Library 23bl; Telegraph Colour Library p56t; Barry Waddams pp13, 55r; Derek G Widdicombe pp3t, 23tl, 39c (Noel Habgood); Hyram Wild p35tr; ZEFA pp3cr, 26, 27tr, 39t, 50, 52l, 56br&bl, 57l.

Illustrations by Julian Baker pp2, 6, 7, 8/9, 16, 17, 23, 24, 25, 28, 29, 30, 33, 36, 41, 42, 47, 50t, 52, 54, 56; Maggie Brand/Maggie Mundy pp4/5, 9t; Joan Corlass pp46, 48; Maltings Partnership pp10, 20, 21, 44, 50, 57, 59; Jenny Mumford p18; Page & Page p40; Karen Tushingham/Maggie Mundy p2, 8, 14, 20, 26, 32, 38.

The publishers would like to acknowledge with thanks the help given by the following people and organisations in the preparation of this book:
Anna Aston, British Shoe Corporation, City of Glasgow Planning Department, Corning Consumer Ltd, Mr G M Dempsey, East Kilbride District Council, The Federation of Bakers, The Flour Advisory Bureau Ltd, Halfords, Ingrid Morrison, National Rivers Authority, Page and Page Architects, Sylvia Scoffham, Hiram Wild Ltd.

Cover photograph: Sydney, Australia
Reproduced courtesy of ZEFA UK.